Whales

by Martha E. H. Rustad

Consulting Editor: Gail Saunders-Smith, Ph.D.

Consultant: Jody Byrum, Science Writer,
SeaWorld Education Department

Pebble Books

an imprint of Capstone Press
Mankato, Minnesota

Pebble Books are published by Capstone Press
151 Good Counsel Drive, P.O. Box 669, Mankato, Minnesota 56002
http://www.capstone-press.com

2 3 4 5 6 06 05 04 03 02

Library of Congress Cataloging-in-Publication Data
Rustad, Martha E. H. (Martha Elizabeth Hillman), 1975–
   Whales / by Martha E. H. Rustad.
   p. cm.—(Ocean life)
   Includes bibliographical references (p. 23) and index.
   ISBN 0-7368-0862-0
   1. Whales—Juvenile literature. [1. Whales.] I. Title. II. Series.
QL737.C4 R87 2001
599.5—dc21

00-009865

Summary: Simple text and photographs present whales and their behavior.

Note to Parents and Teachers

The Ocean Life series supports national science standards for units on the diversity and unity of life. The series shows that animals have features that help them live in different environments. This book describes whales and illustrates how they live. The photographs support early readers in understanding the text. The repetition of words and phrases helps early readers learn new words. This book also introduces early readers to subject-specific vocabulary words, which are defined in the Words to Know section. Early readers may need assistance to read some words and to use the Table of Contents, Words to Know, Read More, Internet Sites, and Index/Word List sections of the book.

Table of Contents

4

Whales are
huge mammals.

Whales breathe air through blowholes.

flippers

Whales have two flippers.

Whales have
two tail flukes.

Whales have fat
called blubber.

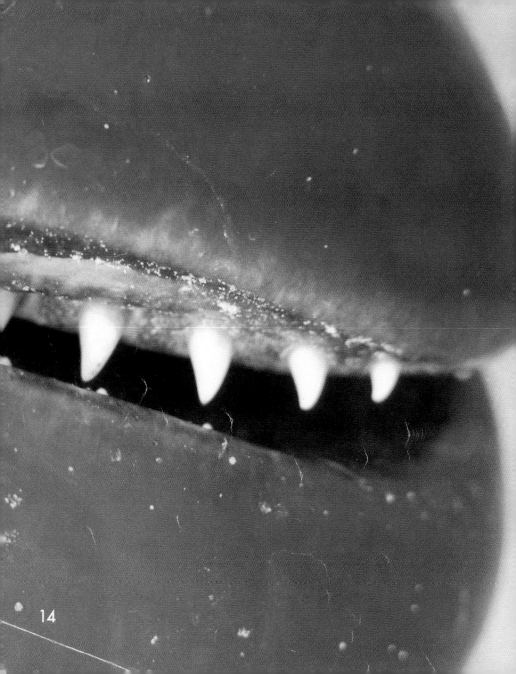

14

Some whales use
teeth to eat.

baleen

Some whales use
baleen to eat.

Some whales migrate from place to place.

Some whales breach.

Words to Know

baleen—rows of fringed plates in the mouth; baleen whales filter water through their mouth to catch fish and plankton in their baleen.

blowhole—an opening on the top of a whale's head; whales come to the surface of the ocean to breathe air through their blowholes.

blubber—fat under the skin of some animals; blubber keeps whales warm.

breach—to jump out of the water; scientists do not know why whales breach.

flipper—a flat limb with bones on a sea animal; flippers help whales balance and steer while they swim.

flukes—the two lobes of a whale's tail; whales move their flukes to swim.

mammal—a warm-blooded animal with a backbone; mammals feed milk to their young.

migrate—to move from one place to another when the seasons change; some whales migrate between warm and cold waters.

Read More

Carwardine, Mark. *Whales, Dolphins, and Porpoises.* See and Explore. New York: DK Publishing, 1998.

Holmes, Kevin J. *Whales.* Animals. Mankato, Minn.: Bridgestone Books, 1998.

Ward, Nathalie. *Do Whales Ever . . . ?* Camden, Maine: Down East Books, 1997.

Internet Sites

Baleen Whales
http://www.seaworld.org/infobooks/Baleen/
home.html

Toothed Whales
http://www.seaworld.org/whalesk3/
toothedwhales.htm

What Is a Whale?
http://www.EnchantedLearning.com/subjects/whales

Index/Word List

Word Count: 45
Early-Intervention Level: 8

Credits

Steve Christensen, cover designer and illustrator; Kia Bielke, production designer;
    Kimberly Danger, photo researcher

Brandon D. Cole, 8, 20
Corel Corporation, 6
François Gohier, cover, 1, 16
Frederick D. Atwood, 4
Jay Ireland & Georgienne E. Bradley, 10
Mark Newman/Bruce Coleman Inc., 12
Robin W. Baird/Innerspace Visions, 18
Visuals Unlimited/Alan Desbonnet, 14